CAMPBELL MORRIS

More Best Paper Aircraft

A Perigee Book

Introduction

Welcome to the world of high performance paper aircraft. This book represents the pinnacle of paper airmanship. Gone are the days of pure aerial fun from the back of the classroom. Now you can create sophisticated paper "machines" — designs that go beyond fun and games to the world of theory and ingenuity, designs that challenge even the most fundamental laws of physics.

Now imagine it's the not-too-distant future, and that you have a career in aeronautics, aircraft building, computer-aided design of space weaponry or shuttle craft. You could even be a pilot flying the new orbital space craft that carries passengers from Sydney to London in less than two hours. The designs that follow this long-winded introduction could be the launching pad for those careers, just as the apple inspired Newton, the flight of birds the Wright brothers and the movement of sub-atomic particles Einstein. So next time your teacher, boss, fellow ditchdigger or mother dismisses you for throwing a paper plane you can reply: "It's my first step to a new career in flight!" (be it as wing commander, astronaut, toilet cleaner, et cetera).

This book is designed to let you think for yourself. It offers first-hand experience in aerodynamics by giving plenty of scope for experimentation and creativity.

You are tomorrow's pioneers. Don't be discouraged by those who say "you can't do it". Some people I know go so far as to talk of a "nuclear Armageddon"; they say, "What's the point of joining the airforce when the very technology that built the Space Shuttle brings nuclear missiles to our doorstep?" But believe me, if you're serious about flight, put aside the negative attitudes. Just think, if we can go beyond the boundaries of our doomsday-minded planet and forget our hidebound ways of seeing, we could reach the endless limits of outer space and so realise the ultimate destiny of the human race!

None of my planes go that far, of course, but I sincerely hope my humble book will give you the inspiration to take to the skies — no matter how old you are.

Happy folding — happy flying.

The Correct Paper to Use

All the aircraft in this book use 8½" x 11" or 8½" x 14" (legal) paper. Make sure you use thin but strong paper. Never use anything like newspaper, which is not strongly bonded and therefore cannot hold a fold. If the paper is too heavy, it might inhibit the more complicated folds shown in this book.

Explanation of Symbols

These symbols are very important if you are to succeed in folding. I have simplified them to avoid confusion. Before you start folding, practise first with small pieces of paper (not money).

Fold in general direction of arrow.

Turn the model over.

Cut along dotted line.

When this valley fold has a dotted line it means that the rest of the fold is hidden behind a flap.

Push in.

Folding Techniques

The technique of folding goes hand in hand with the following of symbols (unless you're crunching up a piece of paper to throw at someone). So grab a small piece of paper and try these tricks:

1.
Valley fold — fold in direction of arrow along the line of dashes.

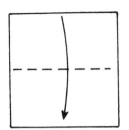

2.
Mountain fold — now fold the top end behind, in direction of arrow, along the line of dots and dashes.

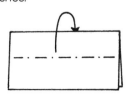

3.
It should now look like this piece of totally useless paper.

Now grab a longer piece of paper and fold it in half.

1.
See the line of dots and dashes? Well, fold along this line backwards and forwards until the paper is well-creased, then holding the lower end A with thumb and finger, push in the other end B to meet the edge A.

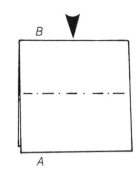

2.
Yes . . . it's almost there.

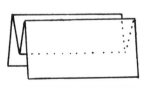

(DOTS SHOW HIDDEN FOLD)

3.
Wow, you got it right! Flatten the paper. You have just completed an inverse fold.

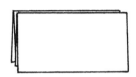

If you want to learn more about paper folding and exchange ideas with other devotees of the art, write to:

Dave Brill
British Origami Society
12 Thorn Road
Bramhall, Stockport
SK7 1HQ England

Despite its name, the Society boasts members in all parts of the world, including the home of paper folding, Japan.

Basic Flight Theory

"Oh yuk" I hear you say — but to understand how your plane flies is a step in making your plane fly well.

There are four basic forces that control the flight of a paper plane (or any plane for that matter). These are lift, drag, gravity and thrust. Lift is a force that pushes an aircraft upwards against the force of gravity. Drag is the normal force of air opposing an aircraft's forward motion. Gravity is a natural force that pulls an aircraft to the ground. Thrust is a force that propels an aircraft through the air, opposing drag. Thrust is created by an aircraft's propeller or jet engine. In paper planes it is created by the motion of your arm throwing the plane.

In figure 1, the kinetic energy of thrust from your arm has propelled the glider in the direction (the intended glide path) you wish it to go. It is met by air resistance — drag — and the glider's lift is temporarily greater than gravity, making it climb. As the kinetic energy expires, gravity overcomes lift and your plane glides to the ground.

Lift is created by a drop in air pressure above an airplane's wing. An airplane's wing has a curved upper surface so that while air moves over the wing its speed increases and causes a pressure drop. The air under the wing remains at normal pressure, so the wing can only go upwards.

The stability and control of an airplane is another factor well worth noting. An airplane has three basic movements: yaw, roll and pitch. A plane makes each movement on an imaginary axis that passes through the centre of gravity.

In figure 2 we can see that yaw is a plane's movement on its vertical axis as its nose turns left or right. Roll is a plane's movement on its longitudinal axis as one wing tip drops lower than the other (figure 3). Pitch is a plane's movement on its lateral axis as the nose moves upwards or downwards (figure 4).

A paper aircraft can have many controls to allow it to perform the way you want it to. Some of these are tail fins, wing fins, rudders, elevators (rear wing lift), ailerons (forward wing lift) and a whole lot more. Refer to the "Advanced Concepts" section to find out more on controlling an aircraft's flight pattern.

I hope this will give you a good idea of what it's all about. These are only the basics and I hope you will take time to visit your local library to find out more on flight theory.

The Art of Throwing

Once you've mastered the folding of paper planes, you'll soon realize there's much more to them than folding — it's throwing that takes real skill. If you want to be the envy of your class mates, fellow politicians, brothers in the church, et cetera, you'll need to be proficient in throwing techniques.

Basics first. You must make sure that your plane can fly straight. This depends on the plane's symmetry. To ensure this symmetry you need to start right at the beginning — with the first fold you make. It is important to fold the model in half either lengthwise or widthwise to get a centerline crease. The best way to do this is to bend the paper over so that the corners meet, and then to spread your fingers across the edge from the center outwards to make the crease.

Each plane in this book is thrown in a different way — and some can be thrown in a variety of ways.

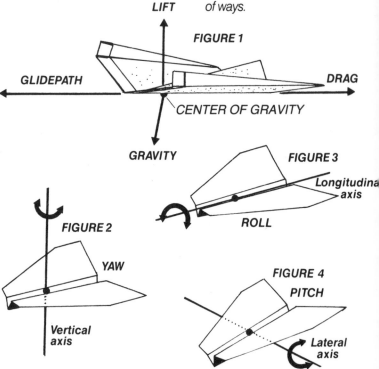

LIFT

FIGURE 1

GLIDEPATH

DRAG

CENTER OF GRAVITY

GRAVITY

FIGURE 3

Longitudinal axis

ROLL

FIGURE 2

YAW

Vertical axis

FIGURE 4

PITCH

Lateral axis

1. To throw a plane normally, grasp the center area of the fuselage with your thumb and index finger, and with your arm move the plane in a forward direction (at the desired speed depending on the type of paper plane selected) and let go. Remember that the wings should be level and that the same level is to be kept until release point.

2. To make your glider loop is relatively simple. Loops are better suited to craft with wider wingspans. By adjusting tail fins or curling up wing ends to give more lift you will have a plane best suited to looping. By holding the fuselage with thumb and index finger and looking down the fuselage with your eye you are now ready to throw. Throw with force (as if you're throwing a rock at someone . . . not that I suggest you do that!) and then let go. It should loop, provided that balance and direction are correct. Sometimes wind direction can alter the plane's looping performance. I suggest you practice and experiment to increase your skills.

3. Some planes in this book are designed to circle horizontally or even in "circle loops" — diagonally — to the ground. Grasp your plane with thumb and index finger near the forward end of the fuselage, the aft end resting against your hand. With the underside of the plane facing your body throw with force towards your left (left-handers throw in opposite motions). Make the angle of attack slightly higher than normal — about 20 degrees above horizontal. It should circle well provided lift, angle of attack and thrust are correct. Practice makes perfect!

Catching upward breezes can be enjoyable. Make a glider with a wider than normal wingspan and plenty of lift.

Looking down the glider from aft to forward, angle the glider at about 40 degrees. By holding the fuselage with thumb and index finger thrust the glider in an upwards arc away from you and parallel to the wind direction. As the glider flies across the wind it gains altitude without stalling and is carried away with the wind. The beauty of the designs in this book is that you can fold a glider in a short space of time from a single piece of paper — so if you lose the glider in flight you can easily make another.

Distance flying is another interesting aspect of paper planes. The right conditions for distance flying (particularly in competitions) are still air and level ground. Darts are better suited initially, but their flight can be interrupted by many things such as turbulence. Darts are great if you have a strong arm and can throw the plane far; but don't be fooled, wider wingspan gliders made by clever designers have achieved great distances. Making sure that your plane flies straight, throw with moderate force in a slightly higher angle to horizontal (about 10 degrees). Keeping your arm straight, let go. Do not throw at a higher angle, as some people counsel, because your glider could stall and dive to the ground — making no distance at all!

Lookouts at tops of buildings or in mountainous areas are ideal for sustained flight. A paper plane can stay up in the air for over half an hour, gently "floating" on air currents as it finally becomes a white dot in the distance. Believe me — I've done it!

Finally, keep practising wherever you are; I've done so for years now and I'm not sick of it yet!

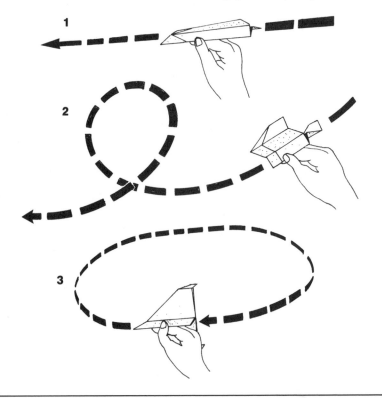

Advanced Concepts in Paper Plane Design

A plane flies or doesn't fly because of its shape. A piece of paper drops to the ground — but it does so in a certain way, wafting in the air in unpredictable directions. It takes slightly longer for a piece of paper to fall to the ground than, say, a brick because the paper is light enough to meet air resistance.

Different paper planes fly with different mannerisms simply because of their shape and what they're intended for. A dart is designed to fly in a certain direction and to meet less air resistance. A wing, on the other hand, tackles air resistance in such a way as to gain lift or perform stunts.

Either way, there are many applications and modifications you can make to a paper plane if for some reason it won't fly the way you want it to, or if you want to "program" its flight path. Here are just a few ways in which you can alter your paper plane.

Concept 1. Fin/Rudder:
This is basically a specialised inverse fold (see "Folding Techniques"). As shown at the rear end of the dart, the fuselage end is pushed inwards, the fold being inverted to form a fin. This can provide lift and produce a more direct flight path.

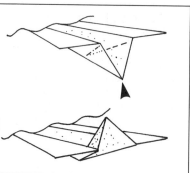

Concept 2. Adding lift to wing/fins:
Simply fold leading edge of fin A downwards; the new flap is now a flat area where air resistance strikes (at the folded angle) giving lift. This is an ideal fold if you wish to make gliders loop.

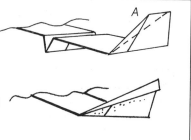

Concept 3. Tail lift:
If your paper plane dives to the ground, or if it doesn't go in the direction you want it to, gently curl up the left tail or the right tail (or one curled up more than the other) depending on whether the dart glides off-course to the left or right (figure 1). This will give the plane more tail lift. If your dart still veers off you can even curl down one of the rear wing tail sections as shown in Figure 2. However, bear in mind that tail lift causes drag and erodes the performance of your glider. A better way would be to start folding a new plane, carefully noting the symmetry of your folds.

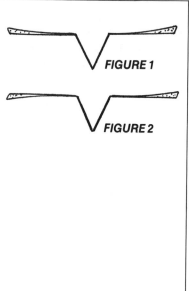

FIGURE 1

FIGURE 2

Concept 4. Horizontally inverted fin:
A novel way to add style and lift to a conventional dart. Cut along dotted line and push fuselage end in and upwards to form fin/rudder.

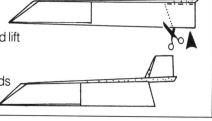

Concept 5. Sealing of fuselage:

This method is used by many professional paper plane enthusiasts who enter their models in competitions. The open part of the fuselage is sealed to give greater speed and agility. The best way to do this is to use a length of sticky tape equal (or slightly less) to the length of the fuselage: fold it in half lengthwise and place it so that the wing edges of the fuselage are sealed together.

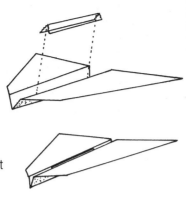

Concept 6. Lightening fuselage tail end for stability:

In many darts, the fuselage is so long that it causes the dart to roll (see "Basic Flight Theory"). By cutting out small sections one can experiment to get the best balance and stability from a dart. Several small cut-out sections rather than one long cut-out section ensure the correct alignment of the dart, eliminating warping.

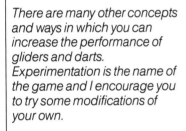

There are many other concepts and ways in which you can increase the performance of gliders and darts.
Experimentation is the name of the game and I encourage you to try some modifications of your own.

Troubleshooting

Won't fly? One way to solve that problem is to light a match to your glider and watch it go down in flames. The better alternative is to go back through all the folding steps as you unfold your glider and see where you went wrong. In many cases it's lack of symmetry. Whatever you fold on the left-hand side of a piece of paper, you must do exactly the same on the right-hand side. It's a good idea to grab a steel rule and measure folds on both sides. In time, you'll be able to judge symmetry pretty well. Other reasons why a paper plane won't fly are:

1. *Not thrown properly.*
2. *Too windy.*
3. *Wrong type of paper used.*
4. *Wrong dimension of paper used.*
5. *Too much lift, too little lift, too nose-heavy.*

Of course, it will take time before you master paper plane technology (and move on to more meaningful things) so take it slowly and you'll thoroughly enjoy every paper plane you make.

Simple Distance Glider

Looks like a dart, smells like a dart . . . but you ain't seen nothing yet! This craft will out-fly any normal glider given the right conditions and folded correctly.

1.
Use a sheet of 8½" x 14" paper facing you lengthwise and fold upwards in half.

2.
Fold down flap — point A should come to rest on folded edge. The distance between B and C should be equal to the distance between D and E (about 5 cm). Do the same for the other side.

3.
Fold flap down so that edge F rests along edge G. Repeat for the other side.

4.
Fold nose down to almost meet edge G. The fold should be from the nose tip to halfway between H and I. Repeat for other side.

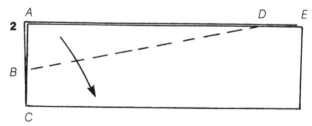

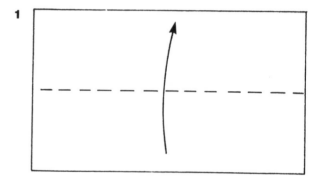

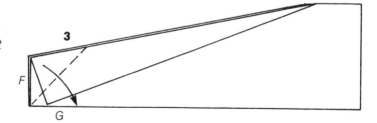

5.

Fold down wing fin parallel to wing edge (to point J). Then fold wing section down to edge G. Folded edge of wing fin (along line J) should come to rest along edge G. Do the same for the other side.

6.

Bring up the wings (to a "Y" shape as you look at the dart head on — which is the case for most gliders) and you are ready to throw.

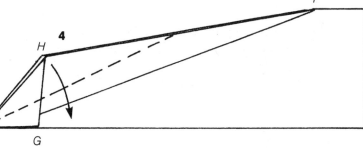

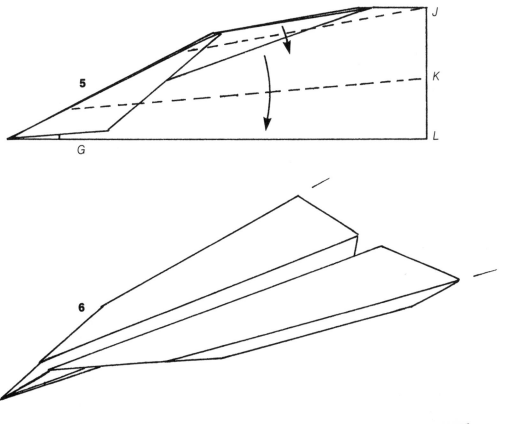

Throwing Instructions

Throw at a level angle to the nearest person in authority. It should glide gracefully. Alternatively you may wish to apply Advanced Concept 5, sealing the fuselage with tape to increase speed — and surprise someone!

Incredibly Simple Glider

This glider is so simple even my mother can fold one! It's a great little glider because no matter where you are you can whip one up in no time to throw at your nearest politician, lawyer, accountant or anyone you happen to dislike at the time!

1.
Fold paper in half lengthwise. See the line of diagonal dots? Bend one corner of your A4 sheet along that line and crease one end, A. This will establish the position of your first fold. Now fold along line AB.

2.
Fold sides in to meet center crease as shown.

3.
Fold nose in so that corners C and D meet edges E and F.

4.
Mountain fold the glider in half.

5.
Fold down the wings in roughly the same position as shown.

6.
Your Incredibly Simple Glider is now ready to throw.

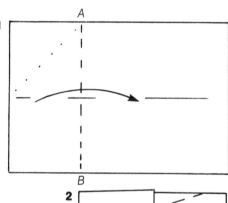

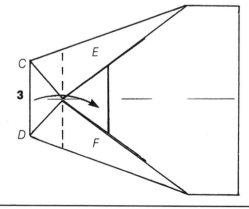

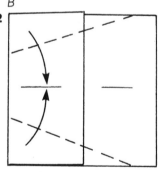

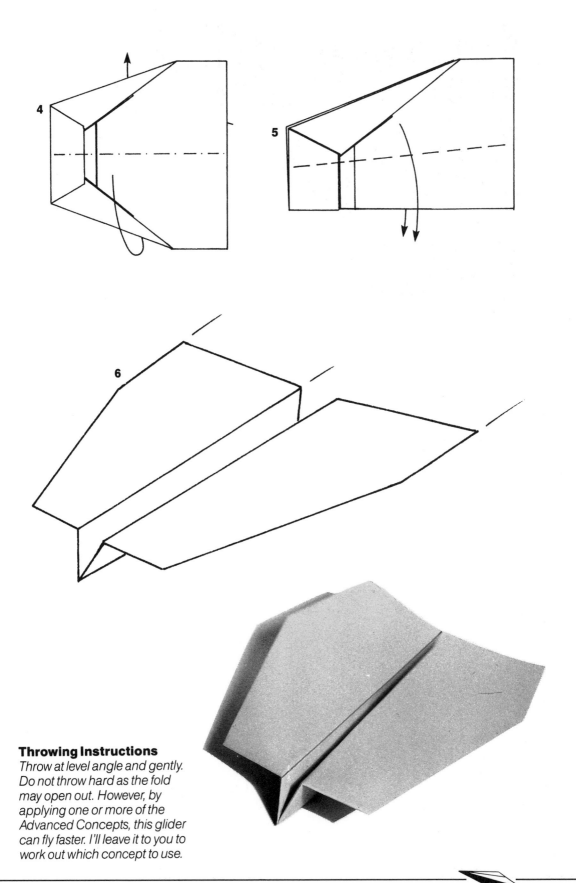

Throwing Instructions
*Throw at level angle and gently.
Do not throw hard as the fold
may open out. However, by
applying one or more of the
Advanced Concepts, this glider
can fly faster. I'll leave it to you to
work out which concept to use.*

Deluxe Glider

A smooth, elegant glider that loves breezes, upward draughts and long, leisurely flights. Once I threw one from a seaside residence and the wind just carried it along the coastline — to finally land in someone's swimming pool!

1.
Fold sheet of 8½" x 11" or legal paper in half lengthwise.

2.
Fold down first flap. Repeat on other side.

3.
Fold down second flap. Repeat on other side.

4.
Fold down wings in roughly level position. You may like to angle about 10 degrees down to nose end if you wish. The fuselage height should be no more than 2 cm.

5.
Fold nose end first, then wing ends up as shown.

6.
Fold down wing fins parallel to wing fold. Give the fins about 2 cm width. Bring wings down.

7.
The completed Deluxe Glider. Add tail lift if necessary.

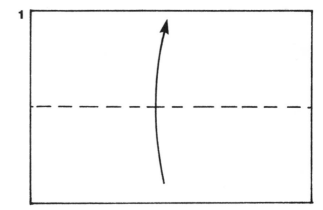

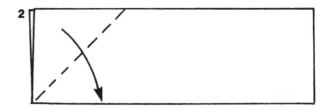

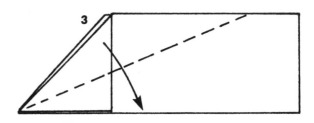

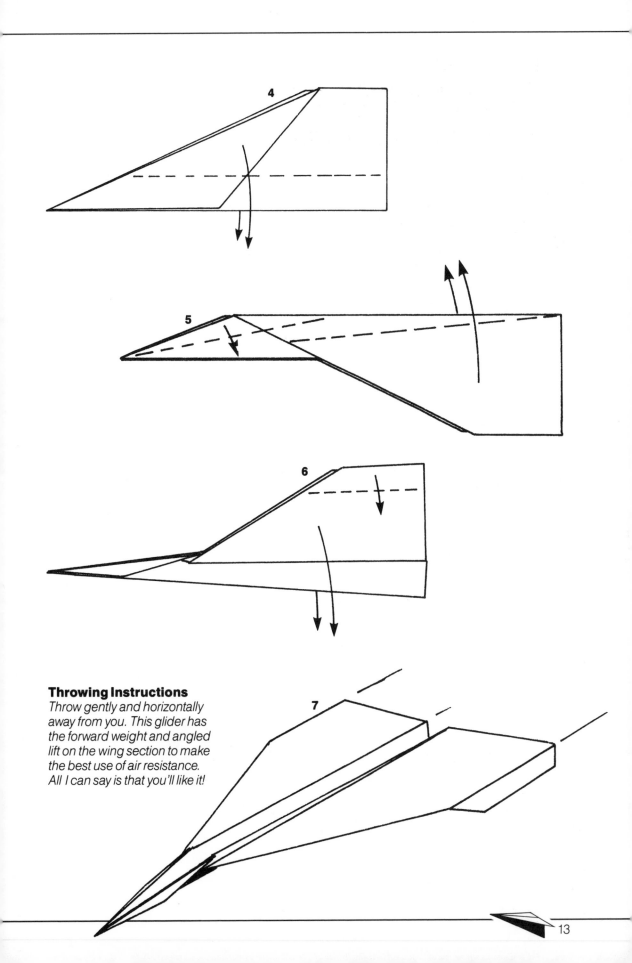

Throwing Instructions

Throw gently and horizontally away from you. This glider has the forward weight and angled lift on the wing section to make the best use of air resistance. All I can say is that you'll like it!

Winged Wonder

A wonderful paper wing that flies so well and is so simple to fold! This glider can really get your head spinning as you try to figure out where it's going to land. Stays up longer in the wind than other wings — and that's due to its large wing area.

1.
Fold sheet of 8½″ x 11″ or legal paper in half widthwise and lengthwise, but crease only the ends and center. You've now found the center of the paper. Fold the top left and right corners in to meet the centre point.

2.
Fold the new leading edges in as shown. Points A and B should meet the top end of the center crease.

3.
Fold tip down to meet point C.

4.
Fold top end down to point C. Then fold along line that crosses point C. This will establish nose weight.

5.
Mountain fold up wing fins along line shown. Fold wing section down. The fuselage height should be approximately 2.5 cm.

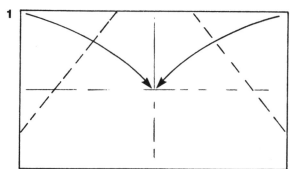

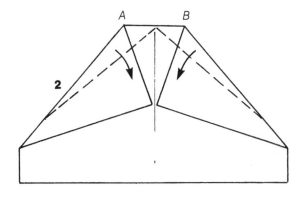

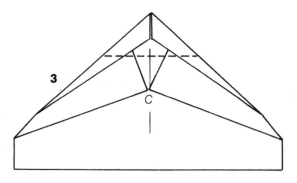

6.

The completed Winged Wonder.

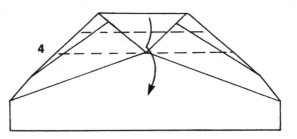

4

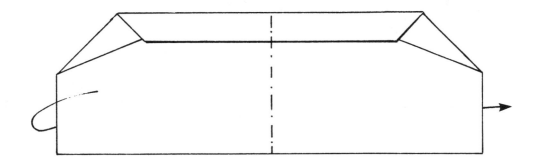

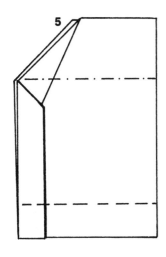

5

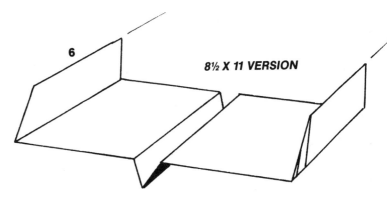

6

8½ X 11 VERSION

Throwing Instructions

It's so versatile! Gently throw forward in a slight downwards angle for a smooth glide. Add a bit of tail lift and you can throw to make loops and circles. Throw harder and upwards. If your Wonder suddenly dives, add more tail lift and refer to Advanced Concept 2 (and maybe others depending on how well you folded the model) to correct the situation. See also "The Art of Throwing".

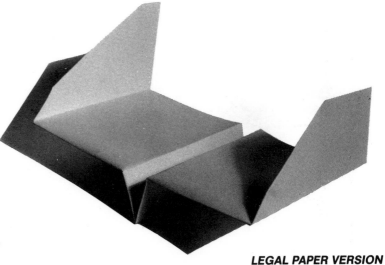

LEGAL PAPER VERSION

Superior Stunt Performer

This craft can do some amazing things. No matter how I threw it it kept returning to me. After doing a stunt, it would often be carried away in the wind. This is a great plane for outdoor concerts. You can write messages on it for your fellow groupies, saying "peace", "nuclear disarmament" or "I hate this awful music!"

1.

Begin with a sheet of legal paper folded in half lengthwise. Fold the end over about six times in approximately 2.5 cm folds each time. This should bring the last fold about half way across the page.

2.

You now have a firm edge of folded paper. Mountain fold the leading edge behind as shown.

3.

Fold in half.

4.

Invert the bottom edge (see "Folding Techniques"). The fold should be from point A to point B which is about 4.5 cm above the bottom edge.

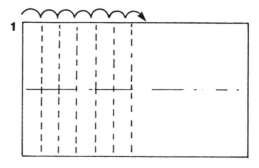

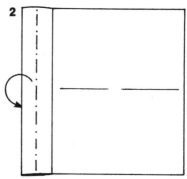

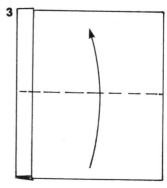

5.

The dots represent the hidden fold from step 4. Fold down the wings, right from the corner of the new tail fin to about 1.5 cm above the bottom forward edge. If you want a smooth graceful glide, your glider is ready. If you want a fast stunt performer, fold up the fins CD in a fold parallel to wing slope giving the forward leading edge of fin about 1.5 cm in height.

6.

Your Superior Stunt Performer is now ready to do its stuff!

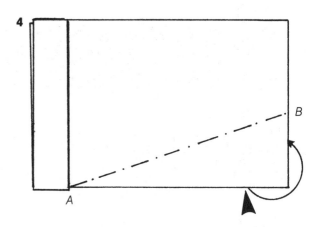

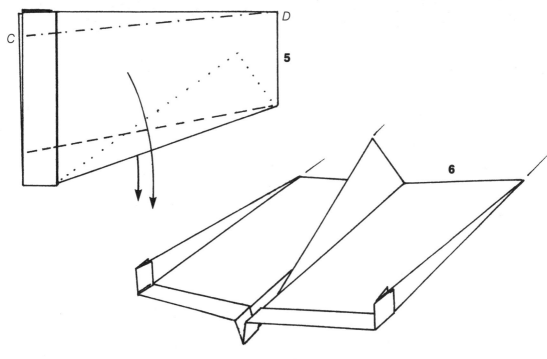

Throwing Instructions

Make sure the folds are well-creased. This glider is more of a circle-looper. As you throw it to make a loop (see "The Art of Throwing") the glider climbs vertically, but just as it reaches its peak it turns sideways to return to you in a diagonal arc. To make a horizontal circle simply throw with force to your left and it will return to you — it's really quite a faithful flying beast!

Distance Achiever

All over the world, politicians are having trouble getting their paper planes (containing leaked information) to the right destination. Very embarrassing when they fall into the wrong hands. I now have the solution to this problem.

    This dart has travelled great lengths and I hope to enter a secret modified version in a competition soon. Fold the dart, enjoy its flight and see if you can modify it to fly further.

1.
Grab a sheet of legal paper and fold in half lengthwise (not you — the paper!).

2.
Fold the corner down to B as in a normal dart, unfold, then fold the corner to the crease DA. Now fold along DA.

3.
Fold down as shown. Do the same for the other side.

4.
Cut along dotted line where indicated. You could use a ruler if you don't have scissors, tearing along the edge of the ruler. I'm so used to making planes, I just fold along the line and tear with my hands. Discard the unwanted pieces (or make little planes if you wish).

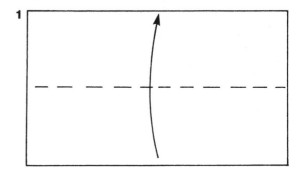

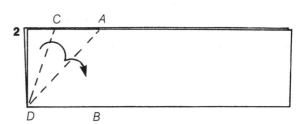

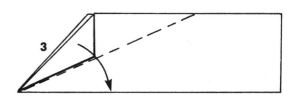

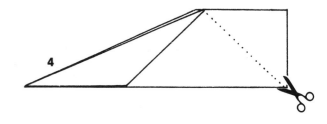

5.

Fold down the wings. Make the
fuselage height about 2 cm.

6.

Fold up wings along fuselage.
You may wish to angle the
wings about 10 degrees. This
step can be ignored if you want
a graceful smooth glide.

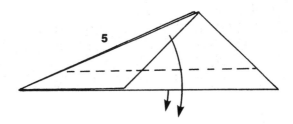

7.

Fold down wing fins and level
the wings. The size of the fin
may need to be adjusted for
correct balance in flight.
Experimentation is necessary.
For better performance, the
loose flaps on the fuselage can
be sealed with sticky tape,
although the craft can fly
adequately without tape.

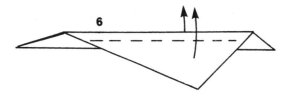

8.

Your finished Distance Achiever.

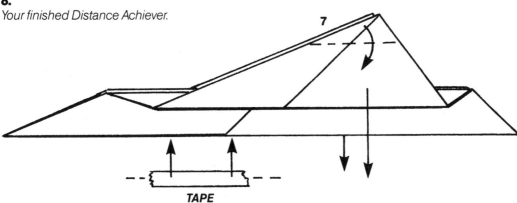

TAPE

Throwing Instructions

For wide arcs, throw as for
circling, but gently. To meet a
required distance, aim and
throw horizontally with a
gentle motion.

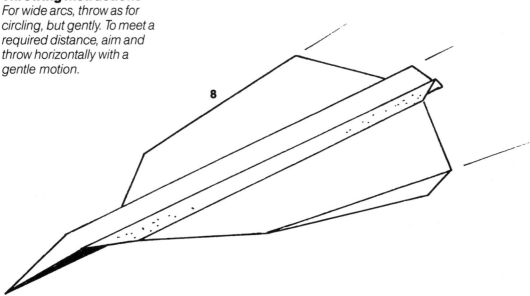

Smooth Flier

Your average, everyday kind of dart is unstable and unsuitable to prolonged smooth flying. Here is another glider that is so simple to make but flies incredibly well — even the teacher will be impressed!

1.
Use a sheet of 8½" x 11" paper folded in half lengthwise. Fold the corners in as shown.

2.
Fold the leading edges in as shown.

3.
Fold in half.

4.
Fold wings down, slightly angled as shown. Give the fuselage around 2 cm height. Both height and angle can be experimented with if you wish.

5.
Fold the leading edge of the wing into a long fin. The fin is shown folded upwards. You can fold the fin downwards for an even smoother flight. See which way you think is best. Bring the wings up for the next step.

6.
Invert the fold. The dots show the hidden flaps inside the fuselage. Where they meet at the bottom edge of the fuselage is point C. Fold your inverted fin from point C to point A. A is the tail end of the wing crease AB. Of course you must crease CA well to invert the fold.

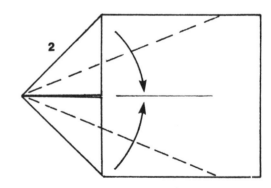

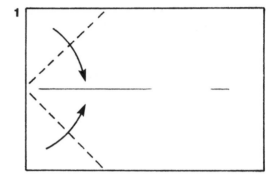

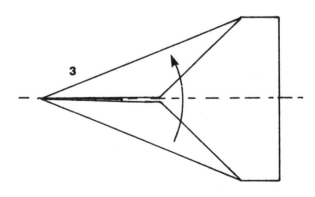

7.

Bring the wings level. The finished Smooth Flyer should look like this. (The fin can be folded downwards as mentioned in step 5.)

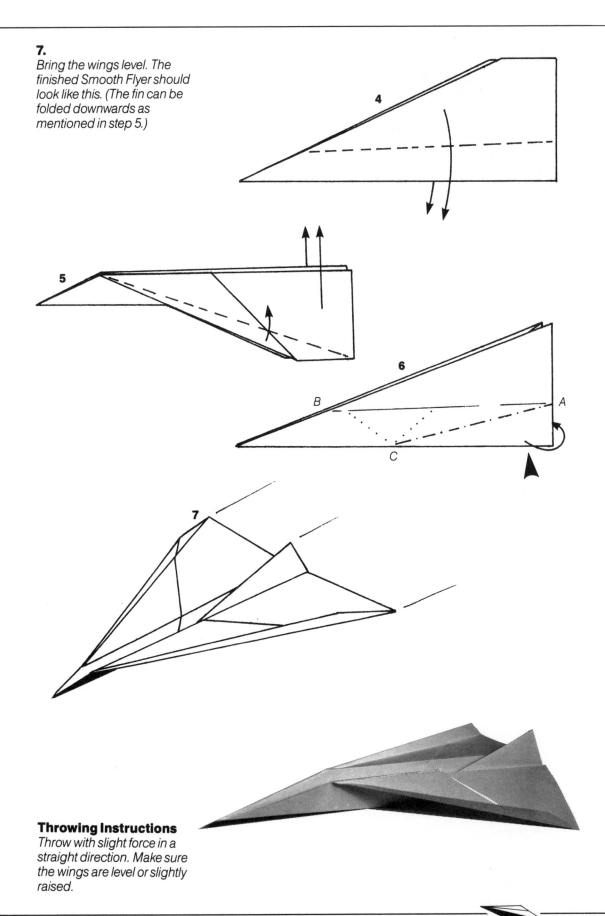

Throwing Instructions

Throw with slight force in a straight direction. Make sure the wings are level or slightly raised.

High Performance Dual Glider

This is actually two gliders in one! I have had never-ending fun with this glider over the past two years as it has so many different flight characteristics. It's the sort of glider I throw at a board meeting or movie; no one knows where it comes from. It must be one of the best gliders I have devised yet, and I mean that sincerely.

1.
Use a sheet of 8½″ x 11″ paper (or slightly less in length). Crease paper lengthwise for the centerline, then fold the corners in.

2.
Fold as shown.

3.
Turn paper over but keep the folded edge A to your left.

4.
Fold corners in again.

5.
Mountain fold in half.

6.
To make the nose cone, fold the top flaps down from inside corner A to corner B.

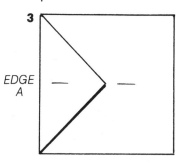

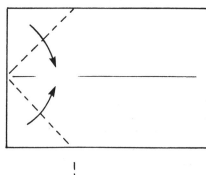

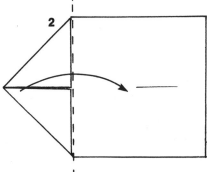

EDGE
A

6½.

The step is half completed as shown.

7.

What it should look like. Here you have the choice to make the glider version or the stunt version.

Glider version: *fold down the fins and angle them so that the fold points to the top point of the nose cone. Fold wings down and angle them slightly as shown.*

Stunt version: *fold up the fins parallel to base of fuselage. Add extra fin lift (if necessary) as shown in Advanced Concept 2. Fold top point of nose cone up, where it meets the wing and fold wings down parallel to base of fuselage as shown.*

8.

The finished Dual Glider — stunt version or glider version. Why not make both?

Throwing Instructions

Glider version: *throw steadily and with some force. The solid nose cone can take considerable thrust.*

Stunt version: *throw to make loops (big ones), circles, arcs etcetera, as demonstrated in "The Art of Throwing".*

Either way, both gliders fly well. Experiment to see which suits you best — you can even combine or change the final folds for some startling effects during flight!

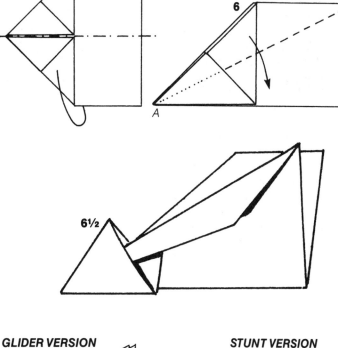

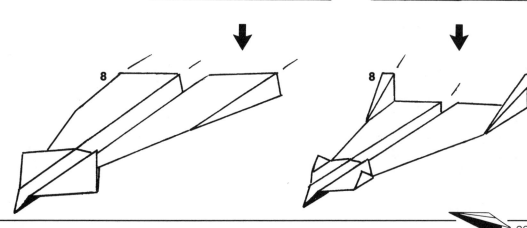

GLIDER VERSION   STUNT VERSION

Not~So~ Simple Glider

Believe me — this may be slightly harder to make but it sure flies well! It features a good distribution of weight and a stability that's hard to match in normal gliders.

1.
Use a sheet of 8½" x 11" paper folded in half lengthwise. Fold the left corners in as shown.

2.
Turn the paper over.

3.
Fold in half — left point folded all the way over to the right-hand edge.

4.
Fold back as shown.

5.
This is what it should look like. Turn over.

6.
Here's the hard part: fold the corner in as for step 1, noting hidden fold, while bringing the nose fold round from behind.

6½.
You're almost there, as shown in this larger diagram. Flatten the fold and do the same for the other side.

7.
It should look like this. Mountain fold in half.

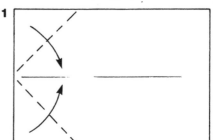

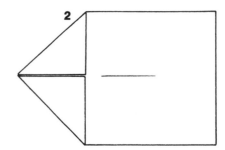

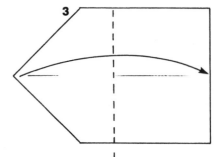

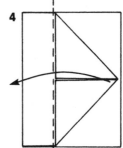

8.
Fold the wings down as shown, slightly angled. Fold the fins down, angling the fold towards the nose of the glider. Invert the tail fin where shown.

9.
It should now look like this. Now that wasn't hard was it?

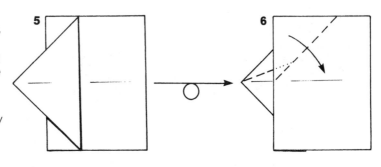

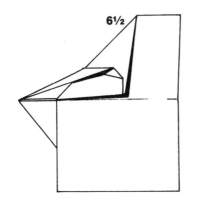

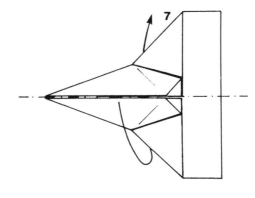

Throwing Instructions

Throw gently away from you for easy gliding. Throw harder, arcing your throw and it will do some amazing aerial maneuvers. I'm sure you'll agree it flies well and is a good plane for practicing folding techniques.

If the nose gets squashed, it can be folded under and back, tucked into a hidden flap on bottom edge of fuselage. You may wish to seal loose folds on fuselage with tape (as with the Distance Achiever).

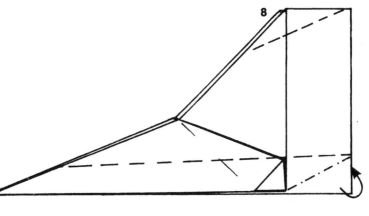

Windcheater

It's a sunny day. You're sitting on a park bench waiting for your loved one to arrive. You see her in the distance and decide to greet her with a paper glider. As you're about to fold, a stiff breeze whirls up from nowhere. The smoke from a gentleman's pipe wafts towards you while the guy to your right lights up a cigarette. Dust is kicked up in the air. Someone breaks wind. "This is too much" you say until you see the nun to your left rolling her own. She strikes a match just as you strike an idea: "I'll make a windcheating aircraft!"

The professors may say "Why is it so?" but I only know that this craft will fly straight through not just moderate winds, but through any kind of pollution. Don't try it in a hurricane though!

1.
Use a sheet of legal paper facing you lengthwise, folded in half widthwise. Fold the corners in normally, unfold, then fold to the crease. Finally, fold over.

2.
Fold tip down as shown.

3.
Fold down as shown.

4.
Fold should be in this position. Mountain fold in half.

5.
Swing your glider around as shown (larger view). Halfway along fuselage cut upwards approximately halfway. See the mountain fold line? Invert the fold along this line but do not crease the line well, A.

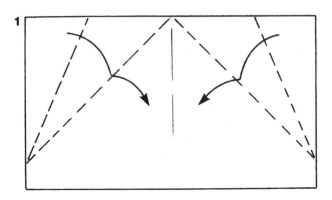

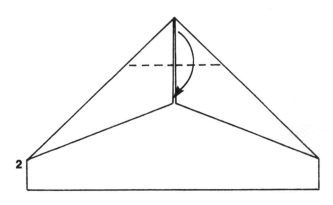

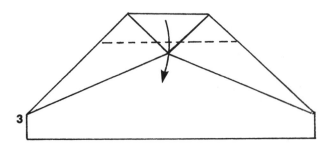

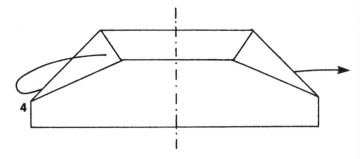